Trans-Formation
In
Everyday Life

A Short Cut to Relaxation and Problem Solving

Kate Cohen-Posey, M.S., LMHC, LMFT

LEIGHTON'S SALES COMPANY

ISBN: 1-885961-00-6
Library of Congress Card No.: 94-78440

Copyright © 1994 by Kate Cohen-Posey, M.S., LMHC, LMFT
Cover Design: Kate Cohen-Posey
Interior Design: Rainbow Books, Inc.
Published by: Leighton's Sales Company
                    P. O. Box 861
                    Haines City, FL 33845
                    Telephone: (813) 956-2998
Retail Price: $9.95

About the Publisher:
Leighton's Sales Company is a marketing firm in the business of selling honey and other products that add to the sweetness of life. Since *Leighton's Honey, Inc.* was established in 1950 to bottle and package honey and due to its expansion through *Leighton's Sales Company* in 1990 to broaden the scope of its endeavors; we will support, produce and market products, programs and policies that contribute to the quality of life and freedom of thought so that today's hardships can become tomorrow's hopes.

Manufactured in the United States of America

Dedication

To
Lela and Harry
and all the
future transformations
that life holds

Acknowledgments

No woman is an island and no piece of writing is born from a vacuum. It would be impossible for me to acknowledge all the great minds who have contributed to this work. Hopefully the bibliography suggests a few, but only a few, because every time I took pen in hand I had an immediate sense of dialogue with the Milton Ericksons, Ernest Rossis, workshop leaders and fellow students who have delved into this subject and have touched me with their written or spoken words.

However, I would especially like to thank . . .

Fred, who took me to my first trance training in spite of myself, before such topics were popular, so my own independent thoughts could ferment over the years before I encountered others' conclusions;

My clients who have been my best teachers and continually inspire me to find the missing pieces in life's puzzles;

The women in the group and other friends who read my writing in its raw form and push me to find my place in the literary market;

And Dana Hilliker, who, as always, used her editorial prowess to make the first read of Trans-formation fit for public view and is slowly but surely teaching me to make my mismatched pronouns agree.

Table of Contents

Exercises

Preface

I first studied hypnosis in 1978. Although I did not use it often, I found it was an essential tool to have in my repertoire of therapeutic skills. I mainly used hypnosis to help clients relax when they were too distraught to focus on their problems and to help them recall details of events they were trying to remember.

In the early 1990's I returned to my formal study of hypnosis to meet the new state requirements for doing trance work with clients. After years of my own independent study and practice many questions came to my mind. I had read research about right brain (RB)/(LB) left brain laterality. I wondered, what is the connection between the subdominant RB and the "subconscious mind" that is supposedly tapped during hypnosis. What actually happens during trance? What physical changes take place? What is the correlation between forms of meditation that had become so popular in the 1980's and hypnosis? Asking workshop leaders questions and further research answered some but not all of my questions.

One benefit I did gain from attending workshops was the desire to use trance more for myself. I had meditated off and on since I was first introduced to hypnosis, but found that there were times when my mind seemed too active to go into trance. Through the process of scrutinizing what was and wasn't being done during training sessions, I realized I needed to TALK TO MYSELF! I couldn't just sit and stare at a spot and wait for trance to happen. I discovered that if I forced myself to get out of bed, sit in a meditative posture and used "directed self-talk" to make predictions of how relaxed I could become and observe changes as they were happening, I could go into trance and gain relief from my frequent bouts with insomnia.

Not only did I find help from long standing difficulty with sleep, but I discovered that when I asked myself questions during trance, I received clear "directions" on how to deal with and let go of life's petty problems. At later workshops I discovered I had fallen into an "inner advisor" hypnotic/imagery technique. I learned other imagery techniques for dealing with physical symptoms and was amazed at how quickly I could get relief from an allergy attack without using medication.

Because I was finding hypnosis so useful for myself, I began using it more with my clients. Whenever possible, I would help people go into trance for a few moments so they could synthesize what they had gained from a session and visualize changes or actions they wanted to take during the coming week. The directions my clients would get from their own inner advisors had the ring of the simple truths I had encountered within myself. Often people had been told what they needed to do about a situation, but hearing it from themselves during trance made a difference. My clients no longer seemed to be people with problems, but, rather, wise persons with a great depth of understanding about life.

Whenever I've found useful information for clients, I've enjoyed writing it in a short, easy-to-read handout. *TRANS-FORMATION IN EVERY DAY LIFE* began as a set of instructions for clients to use to practice going into trance on their own. In the process of writing it I encountered my previous questions about the physiology of trance and discovered my own answers. I have not been able to find research that documents some of my conclusions. These hypotheses are footnoted in the text in the hope that someone with research capabilities will study them further.

I also hope that this booklet can be useful to my colleagues. Some of the therapists who participated in workshops with me seemed tentative in their understanding of trance and apprehensive about using it after 40 or 50 hours of training. Although trance can (and should?) never be completely demystified, the better it is understood, the less intimidating it becomes. Therefore, as much for myself as for others, I've attempted to describe exactly what happens during trance and have added a glossary to assist in the study and further contemplation of trance phenomena. Most of the exercises are written in first person as partial scripts for self-hypnosis and meditation. However, they can easily be adapted by therapists to help people go into trance.

I also welcome experienced hypnotherapists to read *TRANS-FORMATION* to stimulate their own thoughts about what happens during trance and to inspire debate. I believe there are as many ways to induce trance as there are hypnotists. Therapists who have their own style may be uncomfortable with some of the suggested exercises in this booklet. In particular, eye closure, catalepsy and arm levitation seem to be interests of a bygone era. Catalepsy and arm levitation (EX 6, EX 7 and EX 9) help slow down and illuminate the PROCESS of going into trance. Eye closure (EX 4 and EX 5) is an essential experience for people who need to wade into still waters gradually, rather than to jump in the deep end. Therapists who have been trained in more "modern" styles of induction may derive some benefit from understanding the historical techniques from which their own methods evolved.

As with other handouts I've written, *TRANS-FORMA-TION* attempts to reduce the volumes that could be said about self-hypnosis, meditation and relaxation to essential tidbits of information and instruction. Hopefully the material is organized into digestible chunks so the reader can quickly identify areas of interest to read (and reread) and discard the rest. Exercises are given in an order that is useful to the writer, but can be reordered to suit the needs of the reader. Although brief, I hope *TRANS-FORMATION* adds new understanding to an ancient art.

Introduction

INTRODUCTION:

Trans-Formation
In Everyday Life

Anyone reading this book has experienced trance at some time in his or her life. This may have happened while becoming emotionally involved with a T.V. show or sport's game; listening to a moving piece of music; looking at a beautiful sunset; humming a tune that seems to come from nowhere; dancing to the beat with perfect rhythm; or imagining shapes in clouds. A sexual climax cannot be reached unless a person is in an "erotic trance" and an archer cannot make his mark unless he is "*trans*fixed" on the bull's eye. All trance experiences involve concentration, a focus of attention and becoming connected to something whether that be a movie, music, the fragrance of a flower, or your Self. In trance you switch from being a thinker to being an observer. Random thoughts are temporarily shut off, allowing you to become totally involved in your experience.

Trance is impossible when you are in a thinking

modality. At its best thinking is energizing and exciting. Your mind is focused on a particular problem to be solved, stored information is reviewed and solutions emerge from the process of focusing attention and reviewing available information. But thinking is also the source of ALL tension. A parade of "what-ifs," "if-onlys," "when-wills," "have-tos," "coulds," "shoulds," "awfuls," "terribles," "nevers," "always," "nobodies," "everybodies" can march through your mind, literally trapping you inside yourself. Even constructive thinking when overdone can seem to produce a chemical change in your body, making you feel "keyed-up" and making it difficult to unwind and be with others or relax.

It is during such times of tension, preoccupation, rumination and worry that the power of trance needs to be harnessed to break through destructive thinking patterns and to reconnect you to your surroundings or your Self. This book will teach you how to bring under voluntary control what you already know how to do. Simply explaining what trance is and is not and how it is related to hypnosis and meditation will give you the first clues for developing trance. A series of exercises are provided to help you enter trance in a structured way. Finally, ideas for using trance to enhance life and solve problems are given.

What Happens During Trance

During your waking life you are under the direction of the dominant (usually left) hemisphere of your brain. This side of your brain takes in information from your surroundings and inner impressions, organizes them and directs them towards a specific purpose. It helps you make decisions and form judgments. This type of thinking is analytical, active and sequential. Your left brain

(LB) speaks to you through words, numbers and abstract concepts. Although you reason with your LB, its logic can be faulty. Inaccurate conclusions can be stored as tape recordings that get played over and over again to your detriment.

During your dream states you are under the direction of the subdominant (usually right) hemisphere of your brain.[1] Information in this side of your brain is stored as images, symbols, sensations and emotions. Although you certainly have access to your emotions and sensations during your waking life, they are still under the direction of your LB. When you are sleeping your right brain (RB) combines sensations, images, and feelings into dream scenarios that are illogical, disjointed and as real as any thing that happens in your waking life. While your LB helps you navigate reality, your RB dream states may be helping you deal with the impact reality has on you. Dreams are not bound by rules, conscience or even the laws of nature in their efforts to weave current events into the fabric of your past. You may be aware of your right brain taking over just as you drift off into sleep and the quality of your thinking changes.

Whether you are asleep or awake, your mind is always active. After a mentally exhausting day, you can have a mentally exhausting night in which you feel worn out from your dreams. In trance the chatter, chatter, chatter of the LB is brought to a stop. Of course it is not possible to enter trance from a sleeping state, but once the "talking" LB is quieted, it is possible to have access to the images, emotions and sensations of the RB, without the chaotic RB taking over. It is as though when all your brain "busy-ness" slows down, there is something else there that observes, understands and knows.

Exactly what this something else is, is one of the

mysteries of life. Some have labeled it "deep-self," "God-self," "higher-self," "still small voice," "muse," "conscience," "knower," or "peace of mind." To avoid biases and use the most descriptive language possible, I will call this something else the "observant Self." However, if you have encountered this inner presence, you are encouraged to use the term that is most meaningful to you. Because the truths, insights and understandings of the observant Self can be so powerful, some people experience it as "listening to God" and the observant Self may, indeed, be the part of us that can hear God. However, it is not necessary to believe in God to make contact with the observant Self.

When trance is "induced" by an object or activity, you become connected to or totally involved with that event. The surfer becomes one with the wave. The violin and violinist are wed by the "muse." But, when you consciously put yourself in trance, you become connected to your Self — a Self that is awesome in its power. This may be the power to know what is truly right for you, to *trans*cend your worst fear, to remember a painful experience, to block out unwanted physical pain or, in some cultures, to walk on hot coals without being burned. However, this inner power is so quiet and still that its presence is easily missed.

Meditation

The act of consciously putting yourself in trance is called meditation. The word "meditate" is Latin for being moved to the center. During meditation consciousness may literally shift to the center between the right and left hemispheres of the brain. The hypothalamus is in a central area of the brain at the top of the brain stem. It controls arousing and calming responses of the autonomic (involuntary) nervous system. Experiments in which the hypothalamus of a cat's brain is stimulated produce physiologic changes similar to those measured during the practice of meditation.[2] Thus, your calming center is actually in the center of your brain and, although it normally operates involuntarily, you can learn to access it.

Meditation is an age-old practice followed by Christian monks and saints, Jewish mystics, Indian Yogis, Zen Buddhists, Moslem Sufies, Chinese Taoists and tribal shamans. In all forms of meditation thoughts are stilled either by (1) constant repetition of a sound, word or phrase called a mantra or chant, (2) focusing attention on an object or breathing; and/or (3) adopting a passive attitude of observing and allowing random thoughts to pass on. The purpose of meditation may simply be to relax and reverse the effects of stress or to have a mystical experience of feeling the "oneness" of unity with everything, the "no-thingness" of total detachment, or the presence of God. Some people say prayer is talking to God and meditation is listening to God.

Hypnosis

In meditation trance is an end in itself. Hypnosis uses trance to liberate human potentials and bring under voluntary control abilities that normally escape us.

A stage hypnotist may focus on abilities to be spontaneous, silly, or uninhibited. Hypnotherapy can help people re-experience and "correct" painful events, find relief from physical pain, control unwanted habits, solve sleep problems, and discover a host of other inner strengths and abilities.

Although it may seem in hypnosis that a person is under the control of the hypnotist, this is not actually true. The person is always under the "control" of his or her own observant Self. The hypnotist helps a person get connected with his inner Self that knows if it is all right to let go of inhibitions or recall painful memories. It is as though the observant Self is saying, "Sure, I'll play this game as long as you don't do anything I know is wrong for you."

Some people have religious concerns that when your mind is "blank" during hypnosis, you are vulnerable to evil influences. The opposite may be more accurate. When you are not connected to your quiet, observant Self, your LB is easily programmed for desires for power, security and pleasure. These repeat over and over in your mind as "have tos . . . ," "musts . . . ," "needs . . ." If there are evil forces in the world, they attach themselves to this mind chatter. The busy thoughts in your mind are like a crowded train station. An observer in the station would have a difficult time noticing any bad business with so much activity happening. But if the station were empty and quiet, the observer would immediately notice if someone suspicious entered and could sound off an alarm.

Hypnosis is a very confusing term. It comes from the Greek word *"hypnos"* which means "sleep." However, in hypnosis a person is fully alert without interference from random, distracting thoughts. Hypnosis is often defined as a state of heightened suggestibility in which a person will accept *acceptable* suggestions. This suggestibility occurs because the LB with its rules, limits and judgments is toned down. A "benevolent cycle" is created in which suggestions are used to quiet the ever-thinking LB so that the person can become more receptive to suggestions that encourage relaxation.

The suggestions that the hypnotist uses to quiet the

LB (or induce trance) will rarely be as direct as, "stop thinking," or, "let your mind be still." Instead, the suggestions will focus on the process of going into trance and will be much like the techniques a meditator would use. You might be asked to focus on a spot and examine the tiniest details about it; to notice just when *your breathing will start to slow down*; to repeat a comforting word or phrase each time a thought *tries* to enter your mind; to be aware of any thoughts that come to you without placing any special importance on them. The hypnotist talks in a special way to (1) predict trance responses that can happen, without actually telling you to do anything; and to (2) point out trance responses as they start to occur:

> (1) Your body may start to feel heavy, light or detached . . . I don't know exactly how *you will start to feel relaxed* . . . How will you know when *your eyes will want to close?* . . . Don't let your mind become totally still, until you are really comfortably settled in the chair . . . You can try to keep your eyes open, but it may not be worth the effort . . . Your arm can rest on your leg or the sofa as you let go more and more . . . Would you dare to *go all the way into trance* just yet . . . (2) You can notice how still you are becoming . . . The muscles in you face have really ironed out now . . . Your eyelids are starting to feel so heavy . . .

Self-hypnosis uses exactly the same process of inducing trance but instead of listening to a hypnotist you must talk to yourself:

> (1) The first thing I need to do is to focus on a spot

. . . I can remember that that is the only thing I
need to do right now and as I do I will start to
notice changes . . . (2) I just felt my jaw drop . . .
and as it does, my shoulders drop also . . . and my
tummy muscles start to sag . . . Now my eyelids
feel like they want to close . . . my field of vision
seems to be narrowing down and things are
getting blurry around the edges . . . and as my eyes
close and my body becomes so still (1) I wonder
just how still my mind will become . . . I can
count and find out how long it takes before I
need to take another breath . . . and I can count
to find out how long it takes before another
thought comes.

The advantage of self-hypnosis is that you are a much
keener observer of yourself than any other person could
ever be. You can begin making comments to yourself
about changes that are happening more quickly than a
hypnotist could. The trick to self-hypnosis is that you
must continue to talk to yourself and give yourself instructions. If a hypnotist stopped talking to a subject
without giving him any instruction, he would come out
of trance; and if you just sit and stare at a spot and wait
for trance to come, nothing is likely to happen. Just by
talking to yourself, you are shutting off random, mind
chatter and that, in itself, is trance inducing. Listening to
your own directed, focused self-talk acts much like a
mantra. The exercises in this book will teach you everything you need to know about the fine art of talking
yourself into a trance.

Routes to Trance
It is impossible to talk and listen at the same time. In

order to consciously choose to go into a trance, the active (talking) LB must yield to the (listening) receptive RB. It is as though the dominant hemisphere is saying to the subdominant hemisphere, "Okay, I want to go off-line. Watch-out for me, entertain me, soothe me, cleanse me so I can take a break." A balance is created in which both LB analysis and RB synthesis are suppressed. But the LB is aware and has access to RB impressions. It is possible to temporarily suppress LB thinking, reasoning and acting through such RB processes as (1) observing, (2) imaging, (3) relaxing (muscles) and (4) emoting.

(1) OBSERVING: Any trance suggestion a hypnotist gives actually helps a person switch from being a thinker to being an *observer*. Listening to the sound of the hypnotist's voice is an act of observation in itself and helps shut off the person's own random thoughts. In fact, all approaches to relaxation, meditation and hypnosis use this same process of becoming an observer! When you are tensing and relaxing your muscles, you are observing changes in muscular tension. Deep breathing exercises require observation of the process of inhaling and exhaling. Focusing attention on a spot involves visual observation. When you repeat a mantra to yourself or chant, you must listen (auditory observation) to what you are saying or mental chatter will not be stopped. The "passive attitude" of allowing random thoughts to *pass* on is thought observation. Bio-feedback devices help people observe minute changes in skin temperature, pulse rate, and other involuntary body functions.

Senses are the tools of observation. Observations move from the external to an increasingly internal focus of attention. You may start by focusing on an external object, then you start noticing bodily sensations of relaxation and, finally, you sense your eyes wanting to close.

When you "put your body in charge" and allow your eyes to close on their own (without you closing them), you have gotten "out of your head and come to your senses." You have entered an inner realm. This is the place where all true change happens. I can tell you to stop your needless worrying and you may desperately want to let go of a nagging thought, but it will be difficult for you to do so until you have lifted the needle off the broken record that plays over and over in your mind.

(2) **IMAGING:** Fantasy is a powerful relaxation tool that also requires observation of internal images. If you imagine yourself lying on a beautiful, sunlit beach, you are watching a visual image in your mind. Through your imagination you can add sounds, sensations, and fragrances that make your experience more complete. However, if you are having daydreams of power, fame or revenge, your mind is preoccupied with many rapidly occurring thoughts. Day dreams are often goal-oriented scenarios in which you imagine yourself accomplishing some end.

Even when relaxation fantasies involve activity, they focus on experience and enjoyment and are more about *being* than *doing*. Sexual fantasies produce an erotic trance by imagining and then *observing* sights, sounds and sensations that are arousing. They work because they totally shut out random mind chatter which interferes with a person's ability to focus on the sexual stimulation that is actually occurring. Although you may consciously choose the scenario for a sexual or relaxation fantasy, you gradually invite more and more RB involvement as you become absorbed in the image. This creates the RB/LB partnership needed to maintain the necessary balance for trance states.

(3) **RELAXATION:** Whichever route to trance is used

seems to trigger all the other routes. Observation and imagery automatically cause muscles to relax. However, muscle relaxation in itself can promote trance. Motor movement is processed in the LB. As muscles relax, fewer and fewer impulses are being sent, causing the LB to become more passive.

Muscle relaxation imitates the catalepsy that takes place during RB dream states in which muscles are not responsive to commands or external stimuli. Ideomotor movement is the type of muscle activity seen during trance states. Muscles seem to respond involuntarily, move by themselves, or, much like the muscle twitching that takes place during dreams. The tiniest muscle quiver can indicate a whole movement to a dreamer or hypnotic subject. The eye closure and fluttering that takes place as you enter your inner realm is a type of ideomotor movement. Although systematic relaxation of different muscle groups is one way to induce trance, muscle relaxation can occur more rapidly and, possibly, more deeply through focusing and imagery techniques.

(4) **EMOTIONAL RELEASE:** The emotional route to trance is often overlooked and not clearly understood. When you release emotions through talking, crying, laughing, raging, shaking, sweating and yawning, you are also letting go of long-held muscular tensions. If you ever allow yourself to cry, laugh, shake, or rage until all the emotion seems "drained out of you," you can feel calmer and have surprising new insights about your situation. Emotional release has a cleansing effect.

Emotions are not actually produced by situations but by thoughts about situations. Painful thoughts have painful feelings tied to them:

A woman has the thought, 'When my father dies,

I'll be all alone,' which produces actual muscular tension. The muscle tension seems to lock the thought in place. If she had early experiences of feeling alone, the stored tension from those experiences acts like a template creating other perceptions of being alone.

The associations that occur while someone is releasing painful emotions and stored muscular tension are different from our random, waking chattering thoughts. They are like the veins of a mine that lead to the *source* of pain or to resources for healing. The woman in the above example allows her sad feelings about her father dying to well-up in her, making her cry, and she starts to release some muscle tension. As she cries, she has many associations. She has an image of herself in a rowboat about to be overwhelmed by an approaching storm without her father there to rescue her. She is encouraged to let her panic and fear of the storm build, and she suddenly realizes that she has her own oar and she can row herself to safety. She might just as easily have had a memory come to her of being frightened and alone when she was very young. As she released the pain from that experience, she could realize she survived or that she was not actually alone.

The hypnotist uses trance to clear a person's mind sufficiently to begin an "unconscious search" for painful experiences or images for healing. In trance the person can actually relive and release emotions from early painful experiences. But other therapists, without realizing it, are inducing trance by encouraging people to release feelings and allow related associations to surface. As emotions are processed in the RB, getting in touch with any feeling and focusing on it, may help people enter their "inner realm." You may have already discovered that screaming in the privacy of your car or crying is a tremendous tension release. But, some people need a therapist present to help them stay with an emotion and release it fully without getting stuck in a painful spot.

Invitation to the Dance

By identifying trance states that are commonly overlooked, this discussion does not mean to imply that everything is trance. In fact, certain mental states commonly thought of as trance are not that at all. When you miss your turn on the freeway or forget what you came in a room to get, you are likely to be preoccupied. In trance your conscious mind is unoccupied and quiet or open to inner discoveries. Your awareness is actually heightened. A meditative or hypnotic trance will expand Self awareness. But, the African bushman finding his way through unfamiliar territory is in a trance state in which he is totally aware of his environment. A glossary of mental states and processes is offered to summarize distinctions between receptive, unconscious processes and "wakeful," conscious activity.

Furthermore, this discussion does not mean to glorify the RB. Nothing is more exciting than pure thought. Solving mathematical theorems, planning a business venture, or reminiscing about a wonderful evening are the domain of the LB. Trance cannot happen without the awareness of the LB. Should the LB shut down completely, a person simply falls asleep. Interestingly, during certain stages of sleep, when rapid eye movements (REMs) occur, the mind is as active as it is in wakeful states. The brain waves that occur during trance are slower and more synchronized than those that happen when you are either fully awake or in REM sleep. Thus, trance offers a kind of rest that cannot even be obtained from sleep. This does not mean that we should be spending a lot more time in trance, but most of us do need to spend a little more time in trance so we can clear and refresh our mind for its best thinking. And, we need to know how to unlock the door to our inner realm when we need the peace, strength and wisdom that it harbors.

Hopefully this discussion has whet your appetite for the exercises that follow. But if you find yourself bored and lost, do not despair. You may know more about this subject than you realize and have, perhaps, entered trance through the back door . . .

NOTES

[1] *Statements about left-hemisphere directing waking life and right-hemisphere directing dream states are the author's subjective observation. The term "dominant hemisphere" may, in itself, suggest that the LB directs waking states. Although the author is not aware of research documenting this, other facts pointed out in this paper support her hypothesis; i.e.: (1) RB processes tends to be non-linear, disjointed, illogical, symbolic, sensual, and emotional like the activity that takes place during dreams. (2) LB, voluntary motor control is absent in dream states.*

[2] *Dr. Herbert Benson, M.D. in his book, Relaxation Response, p. 96, further describes the work of Dr. Walter R. Hess, Nobel Prize winning physiologist who documents a "trophotropic response" when the hypothalamus of cats is stimulated that is a protective mechanism against over-stress and promotes the restorative processes.*

The Exercises

THE EXERCISES:

Entering Trance

reparing for Trance

When you are first learning to enter trance, it is important to arrange a distraction-free block of time in a quiet environment. Noise and interruptions can be mentally arousing and may interfere with your initial efforts to quiet your active mind. As you become more adept at trance techniques, extraneous noise may not be a hindrance.

After you have chosen a quiet place, you may want to set up an object on which to concentrate. However, any spot or detail can be used for focusing attention. You can even hold up your hand in front of your face and study a spot where two lines cross. Just let you hand gently float to your leg when your eyes close. It is best that you stare at something directly in front of you, rather than looking down with your eyes half closed.

In his book, *The Relaxation Response,* Dr. Herbert

Benson suggests that a comfortable position is one of the basic elements for meditation. Reclining postures in a quiet, relaxed environment often lead to sleep and may not promote the concentration that is needed for trance. However, the key factor in postures that promote trance may have more to do with the alignment of the spinal column than the position of the body.

A tremendous amount of energy is needed to fuel active, mental processes.[1] Much of the energy that gets "caught" in the brain may settle back down into the body as trance occurs. A straight, vertical spine may assist this process. It is possible to go into trance while lying down, but it does help if you are lying flat with your spine straight.

Some experimentation may be necessary to find the best position for you to comfortably concentrate. It is important not to cross your legs in a way that would cut off blood circulation and cause a limb to go to sleep. Sitting on the floor with your back against the side of your bed offers excellent support, helps keep your spine and neck aligned and is convenient when trance is needed for problems with insomnia. A glow-in-the-dark star on the wall makes it an ideal focal point.

Each of the exercises that follows builds upon the previous ones. You may want to do one or several exercises during a practice period. Five to twenty minute sessions are all that is needed to learn to enter trance. Simply do as many exercises as time allows. You may want to repeat some exercises several times and you may feel that you can skip others. Eventually you can establish a routine of the combination of exercises that is right for you. You may prefer to do these exercises with a partner so you can discus your experiences with each other.

Going into Trance

The first set of exercises is something that you have done many times in your life. Only two elements have been added—*will* and *awareness*. By consciously choosing to stare and paying attention to what happens, you will begin to learn many things.

> **EX 1, FOCAL POINT:** Focus your attention on your spot. Concentrate until you sense that you have achieved a . . . **good** . . . **fixed** . . . **stare.** When you are satisfied with the intensity of your gaze, return to the page and read EX 2.

> **EX 2, EYE FIXATION:** Repeat EX 1. This time notice what changes happen in your body simply from concentrating on a spot. Repeat the question in your mind, **"What signs of relaxation am I noticing now?"** After you have noticed one or two changes, return to the page and continue reading.

There are many signs of relaxation you can notice when your body becomes still. It is good to become familiar with them so you will know what to look for. People who are overly sensitized to bodily reactions often worry about any change they notice, especially ones that are different from their usual state of tension. They fear these changes mean a loss of control. However, during trance your mind remains alert, aware and present the whole time changes are happening, even if it feels like you are falling asleep. Likewise, trance is different from unsettling experiences of depersonalization and "spacing out." During depersonalization people feel removed and cut-off from their surroundings and from themselves. In trance you may detach from your surroundings, but you become increasingly connected to your Self. You can come out of trance at anytime you wish; whereas depersonalization is difficult to turn off. The following list of relaxation cues are completely natural, comfortable and good for you:

RELAXATION CUES

Stare becomes fixed	Rate of breathing slows down
Jaw drops (mouth closed)	Some breaths are full and deep
Shoulders drop	Body feels heavy, light, or detached
Forehead smoothes out	Pleasant sinking sensations
Tummy muscles sag	Light, floating sensations
Body becomes very still	Sinuses clear
Face muscles "iron out"	Urge to smile
Eyes blink (slowly)	Eye closure
_____	_____
_____	_____
_____	_____

Some people experience many changes on the list, while others only notice a couple. Some of the signs on the list are complete opposites and could not possibly occur together. Although there are certain commonalties to relaxation, it is a unique experience for each person. You may even notice some changes that are not on the list. Welcome them. The number of changes you notice will have nothing to do with the degree of trance you can achieve. It is important to just allow changes to happen without making anything happen. After reviewing the list a couple of times, continue with EX 3:

EX 3, AWARENESS: Repeat EX 2. As you become aware of the changes that start to happen in your body, use your dire*cted self-talk* to make note of them— **"Now I am aware that . . . (my jaw just dropped) . . ."** Repeat this phrase over and over each time you sense a new development. If you are not sure that any changes are happening, it is fine to just repeat the phrase, **"Now I am aware . . . ,"** or to restate changes you have already noticed. When you sense that you are ready, return to the page and continue reading.

Review the list of relaxation cues. Which ones did you notice? Did you experience changes that were not on the list? You may want to jot these down on the spaces provided.

Eye Closure

If you continue EX 3 long enough, your eyes will eventually want to close. Eye closure is a natural consequence of a good, fixed, stare because the tiny muscles around your eyes become fatigued. When your eyes first close you may notice a brief period in which your eyelids seem to flutter. Along with eye closure, this is a sign of going into and deepening trance. Eye fluttering may be a discharge of muscle tension that builds up from staring. During eye fluttering your eyes may open spontaneously. Just allow them to close again at their own pace. The trick to entering trance is to put your talking/controlling mind aside and allow changes to happen. Eye closure and fluttering is a sign that your listening/automatic mind has become engaged. It is your own personal bio-feedback device that tells you when you are ready to leave outer reality behind and enter the temple of your body. When you are first learning to enter trance, it helps to be aware of the signs that can indicate your eyes are ready to close:

EYE CLOSURE CUES

Eyelids feel heavy	Field of vision becomes narrower
Blinks become slower	Things appear blurry around the edges
Lighting seems dimmer	Funny streaks of light appear
Burning sensation	

However, eye closure can just happen automatically without any prior indicators. It is as though your eyes know what they want to do and do it! Even if you have already experienced eye closure, continue with EX 4 to become more aware of how it happens for you.

> **EX 4, EYE CLOSURE:** Repeat EX 3. After noticing a few signs of relaxation or sensing increased stillness and quietness, ask your Self, **"Are my eyes ready to close, n o w? . . ."** Or, **"Just when will my eyes want to close . . ."** Do not answer this question verbally, but wait and find out what your eyes want to do. A few moments after your eyes close or after repeating the question a couple of times without closure, return to the page and continue reading.

It is really not important whether or not your eyes closed during this exercise. It is only necessary that you ask your Self questions to begin an inner dialogue with your other mind. The process of making predictions and observing what is happening is more important than any outcome. Eye closure can be practiced in a number of ways. EX 5 uses a "back door" approach:

EX 5, EYE CLOSURE: Repeat EX 3. After noticing a few signs of relaxation or sensing increased stillness and quietness, use your conscious mind to intentionally close your eyes. Then ask your Self, **"Are my eyes ready to stay closed or do they want to open?"** Turn you mind over to your body and allow your eyes to answer in their own way. Remember, you are not trying to reach a goal. You are just paying attention to the truth of what your body is telling you. If your eyes do open, simply close them again and find out what they want to do this time. As you continue closing and opening your eyes, there will be many changes to notice, **"This time my eyes seemed to stay closed longer ... For a moment it felt like my eyes were glued shut and then they opened. .. It seems they are ready to stay closed now ..."** After noticing some of the changes that come from closing and opening your eyes or after your eyes have remained closed a few moments, return to the page and continue reading.

It is good to be familiar with both EX 4 and EX 5 as

approaches to eye closure. The beauty of EX 5 is that it helps you begin to notice the difference between the voluntary action of intentionally closing your eyes and the involuntary action of your eyes spontaneously opening or remaining closed. However, staring, in itself, can be such a comfortable, peaceful activity that you may simply want to focus on a spot, observe changes and wait for closure to occur.

Do not be concerned if your eyes open at any time during your practice sessions. Any movement that happens spontaneously is a sign that your are in touch with your automatic/receptive mind. It does not mean that you are "coming out of" trance. Simply let your eyes close again by either EX 4 or EX 5. Opening your eyes and allowing them to close again has the effect of boosting trance. Going into and coming out of brief trances through these structured exercises will, in itself, help you deepen your experience.

Ratifying Trance

It is clear that going into trance is a gradual process and that there is a continuum from light trance states to deep trance states. Trance is not a mind-blowing, peak experience. It can be so subtle that you may hardly know when you have entered trance. The following exercises will help you confirm whether or not you have entered trance. As you can see in EX 7, it is not necessary for eye closure to have occurred for you to have entered trance. But if your eyes have closed you can begin with EX 6:

EX 6, RATIFYING TRANCE: After your eyes have closed, either by the method in EX 4 or EX 5, take a moment to allow any eye fluttering to pass. Then you can have the interesting experience of trying to open your eyes and discovering that they prefer to remain shut. Simply use your directed self-talk to predict this event (called eye catalepsy) and observe it happening—**"My eyes are now resting comfortably shut. On the count of three they can become so tired . . . so lazy . . . so peaceful . . . that they stay closed even if I tried to open them.** *One* **. . . closed and comfortable;** *two* **. . . heavier, limper;** *three* **. . . so heavy, so comfortable, the more I try to open them the more they want to stay closed, and as I stop trying, I can feel myself relaxing more, sinking deeper into my Self."** Do not worry about using the exact script given here. Your own words will come to you. After absorbing this experience you can return to the page and continue reading.

If you have not yet experienced eye closure, you can use EX 7 to confirm that you have entered trance by creating an arm catalep*sy*. As defined in the glossary "catalepsy" means that your muscles do not respond to ordinary commands. In EX 7 your receptive, illogical RB can defy your conscious intention to lift your arm:

EX 7, ARM CATALEPSY: Rest your hands comfortably on your thighs and choose a spot on one of them to focus your attention. As in the first three exercises, (1) build a good, fixed, stare; (2) ask your Self what signs of relaxation you are starting to notice; and (3) observe any of the changes that you do notice. After you have sensed an inner quiet and stillness you can begin your directed self-talk to predict arm catalepsy— **"My arm is now resting comfortably on my leg. On the count of three it can become so tired ... so lazy ... so limp ... that it would not lift even if I tried to move it.** *One* **... relaxed and loose;** *two* **... heavier and limper;** *three* **... so heavy, so comfortable, the more I try to lift it, the harder it is to move, ... and as I stop trying, ... I let go even more ... my eyes close and I sink more deeply into my Self."** Again, do not be concerned with using the exact script given here. After you have absorbed this experience you can return to the page and continue reading.

Creating catalepsy is a totally illogical experience.

Suggesting that a muscle cannot move and telling it to move at the same time is confusing and increases your receptivity to suggestion. However, be assured that at any time during trance that you need to move, you can easily do so without the hindrance of contradictory suggestions. Catalepsy offers a way to (a) practice bypassing the logical, rule-bound conscious mind, and (b) ratify that some degree of trance has been entered.

Review

The first five exercises are all that you need to put yourself in trance.

As you become more familiar with trance, you will not find the need to confirm your experience and you may not want to include EX 6 and 7 as apart of your routine. This booklet does not offer a static, one-two-three formula for relaxation. Going into trance is a dynamic process that can change each time you do it. As long as you are (1) using self-talk to guide and direct yourself and (2) "listening" to inner responses, trance will come. The following self-talk script is offered as an example of one way to combine the previous exercises.

EX 8, REVIEW: (Ex 1) "All I need to do right now is concentrate on my spot. Even the words I use to talk to myself are not really important . . . my concentration is all that matters . . . now my eyes do seem to be locked on my spot . . . and **(Ex 2)** I wonder what signs of relaxation I will start to notice first . . . **(Ex 3)** Now I'm aware my jaw just dropped . . . and I took a nice deep breath . . . my tummy muscles are letting go and my face feels all ironed out . . . now I'm getting that clearing sensation in my nose . . . **(Ex 4)** And I wonder when my eyes will want to close . . . I'm blinking sort of slowly . . . **(Ex 5)** I think I'll go ahead and close my eyes and find out if they want to open . . . it feels so nice to just let them close and open on their own . . . and they're staying closed longer and my body feels so heavy . . . and now they're closed and the fluttering is going away . . . **(Ex 6)** I wonder if I could let them get so lazy that it wouldn't be worth the effort to open them . . . *One* . . . closed and comfortable; *two* . . . glued shut; *three* . . . so heavy, so peaceful . . . the more I try to open them the more they want to stay closed . . . and now I stop trying and I feel myself becoming limper . . . looser . . . all over and at peace . . ."

As you become more familiar with trance, the above induction will become shorter and shorter until you find your eyes seem to close just moments after you focus on your spot. When you are "wound-up" it can be helpful to have a longer induction because it forces you to concentrate on the process of going into trance. The following exercise offers a script for a "hand levitation." During a hand levitation your arm will seem to float off your leg. This happens through *ideomotor* muscle movements in which muscles respond involuntary to your observations and predictions. An arm levitation is an excellent way to practice using self-talk to (a) make predictions of a desired change, (b) break down the change into the tiniest units possible and list all the ways each little change could happen, and (c) notice changes as they occur:

EX 9, ARM LEVITATION: (a) "It would be interesting to find out just how my hand would float off my leg . . . as I stare at my hands I wonder how I will first notice my hand wanting to move . . . **(b)** will I see a tiny stirring . . . a twitch . . . or will I just feel it . . . **(c)** I seem to be narrowing my focus on my right hand . . . and I feel a pulling in my right forefinger and it is turning ever so slightly off my leg and it is pulling my thumb with it . . . and now it and my thumb are suspended a fraction of an inch off my leg . . . and my hand is turning more and more so that only the side of my hand and my baby finger are resting on my leg . . . and **(a)** I wonder how my hand will actually float off my leg . . . **(c)** but I notice my arm is pulling back and my hand is suspended just the tiniest bit above my leg . . . it seems to stay still there but with each breath I take, my hand makes the tiniest movement as though my breathing were a pump lifting my arm . . ."

It is possible to use self-talk to levitate your hand until it touches your face. It will seem for brief periods that your hand or arm is stuck in space as though it could move no higher and then your automatic, suggestible mind will find a new muscle group to contract that pulls your hand further in its path towards your face. During these periods of suspension you can predict, **"I don't**

know just where my hand will touch my face, but when it does, my eyes can close and my arm fall limply onto my lap as I drop all the way into a pleasant, peaceful trance." Trance suggestions can always be made in a no-lose way. If after a few predictions and careful observation your hand makes no movement off our leg, simply say, "**My arm seems to be telling me it doesn't want to move and, if I even tried to move it now I might find that it had become too lazy to make the effort . . . and as I stop trying, I let go, close my eyes and go all the way into my Self.**"

Although hand levitation can seem dramatic and showy, its main value is a vehicle to practice self-talk and concentration. The feeling of detachment that can happen during levitation can also be helpful for those working with pain control. EX 9 is entirely optional. Developing your own style and comfort with EX 8 is more important at this point.

Problems Going into Trance

Initially, it is good to practice relaxation skills at times when you are not facing a particular issue. However, it can actually be easier to go into a trance when you are tense or upset, because a part of you craves the peace and solitude it offers. However, there may be times when it is difficult for you to achieve the level of concentration you need for trance. The following discussion points out a few common problems and offers suggestions:

1. **EXCITEMENT** can cause your mind to race. It seems to go from one thought to the next and then off on tangents. As soon as you start to focus on a task, you are distracted. You may not even have the will to want to

enter trance because you are enjoying your thoughts so much, but you know if you don't settle down, you won't be able to sleep or concentrate on the task at hand. At these times you may need to force yourself to write down every thought you are having or do your self-talk out loud. Making yourself read something boring can also help. Reading is a good precursor to trance because you start to focus on thoughts other than your own. Singing a song, watching TV or listening to music can have a similar effect. Dancing has the advantage of releasing excess energy built up from excitement. As soon as you sense that your thoughts have slowed down enough to give you the will for firm, loving, directed self-talk, you can start your induction.

2. Being **OVER-WORKED AND OVER-TIRED** can also produce racing thoughts. Making yourself do tedious, mindless work like scrubbing a floor can help. Many of the suggestions for excitement offer good transitional activities that can help you unwind. The Metaphor of the Mind on page 89 was designed to help you gear down when your mind is over-worked. EX 13 and EX 14 in the next section teach breathing techniques that can help you prepare for trance, as well as maintain trance.

3. It can be difficult to go into trance on top of **INTENSE EMOTIONS.** As stated on p. 6, Emotions are spontaneous, physiological reactions to thoughts that are processed in the RB. When emotions are held in, they seem to lock distressing thoughts in place in a way that causes them to repeat over and over in your mind. When you start to discharge emotions through talking, laughing, crying, shaking, etc., not only is tension released, but spontaneous associations occur which lead to sources of pain and resources for healing. Focusing on the physical sensations that accompany emotions is much like other trance-inducing activities of noticing changes that occur in your body. Giving voice to repetitive, controlling thoughts helps dislodge them to begin the healing process.

More specifically, expressing sad feelings to an image of a person or object you have lost can help you cry and even sob. Throwing darts, pounding on your bed or screaming into a pillow are safe ways to let go of anger. Surprisingly fear can be released through laughter. If you're afraid of losing your job, practice begging with a tin can. Say your worst fears out loud with your nose pinched. Once some emotional energy has been drained off, it can be easy to slip into trance. Reading inspirational material, a favorite poem or the Bible is a good transitional activity that can help you turn loose of negative thinking and prepare to quiet your mind.

Stephen Wolinsky in his book *Quantum Consciousness,* has meditation exercises for working with "E-motions" in which you (1) notice where the emotion in your body is occurring; (2) take all your attention off the cause or thoughts associated with the feeling; and (3) focus entirely on the bodily sensations themselves, de-labeling them and seeing them as pure energy. Remarkably, he states, this exercise can produce a profound change in which the distressing emotion "transmutes" into a deep sense of "peace, comfort and bliss" and leads to higher states of expanded knowledge. This method may be very helpful when you are unable to discharge emotions.

4. INTENSE PAIN can interfere with the attention you need to go into trance. However pain can actually be an asset for trance. A discussion of EX 22 on p. 78 describes how this can work. As you become absorbed

in Exercise 22, you may find yourself entering trance or
reaching a level of comfort that allows you to begin other
trance enhancing exercises.

    **5. ATTENTION DEFICIT HYPERACTIVITY DISOR-
DER (ADHD)** is a neurological condition that makes
focusing attention very difficult. It is commonly thought
of as a childhood problem. However, there are adults
who are affected by ADHD even though they have man-
aged to compensate in many ways. The stillness that
comes from focused attention is very pleasant for most
people. Hyperactive people have a "paradoxical" reac-
tion to stillness that makes it unsettling. They seem to
"fight" focusing attention with muscle twitching and
fidgeting. There are medications that are enormously
helpful for people with ADHD and a medical consult
should be sought if it is suspected. It may be easier for
people with ADHD to attempt the exercises in this book
while sitting in a rocking chair or even pacing.

    Although the above problems can occur, with prac-
tice you will find ways to work through most any mental
state you might have and discover that going into trance
is a very easy, natural process. But this is only a beginning. Once in trance you will want to learn how to
deepen it, maintain it and use it as a resource for facing
life's problems. The next set of exercises offers direction
for how to settle into your inner realm once you have
entered it.

NOTES

    [1]*Beta brain waves that occur during states of mental arousal
are usually 13 to 25 cycles per second but can be as high as 50
cycles per second. The alpha waves that occur during periods of
rest and trance cycle at a frequency of 8 to 13 per second and may
reflect the marked decrease in energy utilized by the brain cortex
during these states.*

Maintaining Trance

rounding

Much of the language of trance suggests a downward movement — "going deeper and deeper," counting *down* from five, walking *down* steps, etc. Some approaches to meditation would explain this as the need to "ground" energy and establish an "energy connection" with the earth. When energy is not "grounded" it (supposedly) degenerates into nervous tension and irritability. Once energy is grounded a reciprocal relationship is established in which energy flows up into a person from the earth. Many tribal dances use a step in which the feet are alternately lifted part way off the ground as though pulling energy up out of the earth.

While such ideas can be difficult for our western minds to grasp or validate scientifically, they do offer useful images to help deepen trance and explain sensations of sinking or floating. Imagining energy retreating from the outer cortex, moving toward the base of your brain and down your spinal column into the earth is a metaphorical reason for the pleasant sinking sensations that can occur during trance. Likewise, picturing energy flowing up from the earth, filling you and lifting you can increase any light, floating feelings you are having. Grounding is helpful after you first enter trance to "anchor" your experience and help you stay where you want to be.

EX 10 and EX 11 employ counting techniques and images commonly used to deepen hypnotic trances. Understanding that these methods are a means to begin grounding can further their effectiveness.

EX 10, GROUNDING: After entering trance through your own version of EX 8 or EX 9, simply count down from 5. With each count you can imagine loving hands pushing down gently on your shoulders, teaching your body something else it needs to know about going all the way into trance. Or, you can visualize going down steps, an escalator or elevator with each count. Be sure to use your self-talk as you count: *"Five . . .* **I'm ready to start sinking downward as I imagine a lovely, gentle pressure pushing on my shoulders . . .** *four* **. . . I go a few more steps deeper down and feel my shoulders dropping . . .** *three* **. . . descending further and further into my Self . . .** *two* **. . . drifting down a few more steps with that gentle pressure helping me . . .** *one* **. . . go all the way inside where it is peaceful, comfortable and still."**

If you have ever tried to touch the bottom of a deep pool of water, you may have noticed it takes several bobs up and then more pushing down before you gain the momentum to reach your goal. EX 11 uses this idea to deepen trance.

EX 11, DEEPENING: After counting down as you did in EX 10, start counting upwards to bring yourself out of trance: **"And now that I'm all the way down in my comfortable place, I can begin floating right back up again . . .** *two . . . to a more alert . . . three . . .* aware *. . . four . . .* **outward state and now . . . my eyes open and I'm present but relaxed and aware of everything I've just experienced . . . as I let myself sink right back down . . . my eyes close** *. . . four . . .* **I go back down those steps** *. . . three . . .* **those lovely hands pushing me lower . . . deeper** *. . . two . . .* **further down until** *. . . one . . .* **I'm even deeper inside my Self . . . and I memorize and absorb just what I'm experiencing . . . wondering . . . just how deep I can go each time I ascend and descend the stairway into my Self . . ."** You may want to repeat this bobbing into and out of trance several times before going on to other exercises. As you do this exercise, it can help if you let one of your fingers float up as you bring yourself out of trance and slowly fall back down as you go back into trance.

EX 10 and EX 11 focus on the downward movement of energy to begin the process of grounding. EX 12 adds imagery and the element of connecting with the earth to enhance this process. It is best done in a sitting position:

EX 12, GROUNDING IMAGERY: After entering trance, use your self-talk to study how your body is balanced— **"My head is perfectly balanced on my neck"** (If your head begins to droop, imagine a string coming out of the center of your head, holding it in perfect alignment with your neck.) **"I can feel the weight of my head resting on the top of my spine. I notice how that weight is carried down, one vertebra at a time, all the way down my spine . . . and I can feel that weight pressing down on the floor (chair) I'm sitting on . . . and through the force of gravity, the earth is pulling my weight towards it . . . all the way through the sub-structure of my house (even if I am in a high rise) . . . to the very center of the earth itself . . . so I can imagine and almost feel the column my weight makes as it bores its way into the earth . . . allowing the excess energy from my outer brain to move through my body (replenishing and nourishing it) and then descend all the way to the core of the earth . . . to an unlimited source of pure energy that can rise through me . . . buoying me . . . lifting me . . . allowing me to move through life with grace and ease . . ."** Do not attempt to use this exact script during your own trances. As you read it now, simply understand and visualize it so that the words that are just right for you will come to you when you want them.

There are as many ways to ground energy as there are images in your mind. You may want to think of your spine as the trunk of a tree with roots extending into the earth. Or, if your are lying down, you can think of yourself as a body of water, seeping through the earth to the aquifer below. An unlimited variety of stairways, escalators, elevators, air shafts, wells, poles, etc., are available to help you descend to the very deepest part of your self and discover the connection you have to some ultimate substrata below.

Centering

"Centering" is a common term used in meditative practices. "Meditate," itself, means (in Latin) to move to the center. Trance is achieved through a sort of mental "teeter-tottering" in which LB analyzing is suppressed while RB observing increases until a balance is reached. When you come to the middle of your inner "see-saw," you are poised over your center of gravity and aligned with the openings of both of your minds (RB/LB). As mental activity shuts down, stored information, impressions and inner truths become available.

Centering begins when you adjust your posture and focus on a spot. As your eyes close (on their own), you enter the middle ground between your outer and inner minds. But, to stay in trance, you must remain balanced and centered to keep from falling back into waking (or sleeping) thought patterns. You come to rest in the quiet and stillness of your "no-thought" place. The very center of your center is an infinite and unexplored territory. A spiritual text called *A Course in Miracles*, p. 360-361, describes it beautifully:

"Mind reaches (in)to itself . . . Within itself it has

no limits . . . The body is outside you, shutting you
off from others and keeping you apart from them
. . . You (can) reach beyond the body, but not
outside yourself . . . and experience . . . a sense of
being transported beyond (yourself) . . . This
feeling of liberation . . . entails a sudden unaware-
ness of the body, and a joining of yourself and
something else . . . The body . . . does not limit you
. . . You are not really "lifted out" of it; it cannot
contain you . . . In these instants of release . . . you
experience the lack of awareness of the body . . .
You come to this place of refuge, . . . through . .
. a quiet melting in.

Thus, centering yourself is not a static goal, but an
ongoing process in which you find some "black hole" in
your mind where you can travel endlessly into, and
perhaps, beyond yourself. The exercises that follow
offer several techniques that can help you remain centered while you are on your journey.

The first step on this voyage is as simple as breathing.
Breathing offers an inner focus of attention after your
eyes have closed and you can no longer see your spot. EX
13 - EX 15 offer several different approaches to aware
breathing. You can first do them while reading the
exercises. When you learn the techniques, they can be
done after you have entered trance, or as a preparation
for trance.

EX 13, COMPLETE BREATH: This technique can be broken into four steps: (a) Begin with a very slow, quiet inhalation through your nose. Simultaneously, push out your abdominal area. This movement allows air being inhaled to enter lower into your lungs. (b) Continue to inhale and expand your chest to allow air to enter the upper area of your lungs. (c) Hold your breath for a count of five. (d) Now exhale slowly through your mouth. When your exhalation is completed, repeat a couple of times. While in trance, use your directed self-talk to guide yourself through this exercise: **"(a) First I bring air all the way down into my tummy ... (b) then I let air fill up my chest ... (c) now I hold for five counts ... (d) then I release air all the way as I *let go* ..."**

The COMPLETE BREATH is a basic Yoga practice. Its primary purpose is to use your lungs in their entirety in order to extract as much "life force" as possible from the air. It is a wonderful feeling to allow your lungs to stretch to their full capacity. When your muscles pull down your diaphragm (membrane between the lungs and abdomen) to take a deep, satisfying breath, you are breathing from your center. This can seem awkward at first if you are used to using only a small portion of your lungs for breathing.

You may want to do this exercise once or several times until it feels natural. It leads nicely into the slow, rhythmic CLEANSING BREATH that further enhances relaxation.

EX 14, CLEANSING BREATH: This exercise is also done in four steps: (a) Inhale through your nose for three counts, (b) hold for three counts, (c) exhale through your mouth for six counts, (d) pause for three counts . . . repeat two more times. Your self-talk will consist mainly of counting: "**(a) Breath in . . . *one . . . two . . . three . . .*, (b) hold . . . *one . . . two . . . three . . .*, (c) breath out . . . *one . . . two . . . three . . . four . . . five . . . six . . .*, (d) pause . . . *one . . . two . . . three . . .*"**

The CLEANSING BREATH actually alters body chemistry. Inhaling to the count of three brings oxygen to the brain and feeds cells throughout the body. Exhaling to the count of six expels carbon dioxide and relaxes muscles. Thus, the cleansing (exhaling) phase of the breathing cycle can double and even triple the stimulating (inhaling) phase. Inhaling through the nose avoids drying throats and exhaling through the mouth helps control and slow down the release of air.

Holding your breath for three counts before exhaling can help reduce the tendency to feel light headed. After you become familiar with the CLEANSING BREATH it is no longer necessary to count while exhaling. EX 15 helps you tune into the natural rhythms and needs of your body.

EX 15, CLEANSING BREATH: As in EX 14, breath in for three counts and hold for three counts. When you exhale and pause, simply wait until your body needs to take another breath. While you are waiting, you may want to ask yourself a couple of times, **"Do I need another breath yet? . . ."** Pay exquisite attention to how your body tells you when you need to inhale. What else do you notice during the exhaling/pausing phase? You may become aware of your heart beat or an inner sense of rocking.

Exercise 16 uses an image from Kay Cordell Whitaker's book, *The Reluctant Shaman,* p. 62, to help sustain attention on your breathing.

EX 16, BREATHING IMAGERY: See yourself in a lovely warm (cool) sparkling pond of water. Use your self-talk to guide yourself through this fantasy— **"I am submerged up to my lips. I can hear birds and insects and teeming life and feel the mud squishing through my toes. A leaf falls in front of me. As I breathe in, the leaf floats to me. When I breathe out, it floats away. I watch this leaf come back and forth until it seems that the leaf is a part of me and that I am a part of it."**

During the CLEANSING BREATH, your breathing slows down so that you are taking fewer and fewer breaths a minute. This has a profoundly calming, peaceful effect. But, even as you retreat further into the quiet of your center space, you may notice occasional thoughts wanting to intrude. EX 17 gives you a tool to block any thoughts that might try to pull you away from your center.

EX 17, MANTRA: After entering trance, grounding and cleansing through one of the breathing exercises, take a moment to notice your experience. Memorize what this level of relaxation feels like. Ask your Self for a word, phrase, sound or image that describes how you feel in your center space– **"What picture, color, word, phrase, sound . . . represents what I'm experiencing now? . . ."** Wait for an answer to come. Silence is a wonderful answer in itself, but it is fine to repeat the question a few times to help you listen to truths from within. Learn to distinguish "talking thoughts" from ideas realized through a quiet "knowingness." You may see the color blue or a purring cat; or "hear" the word "quiet," "still," "clear," "laughter," "noodle," a phrase from the Bible or a familiar tune. You may even smell a fragrance or feel a refreshing breeze. Accept whatever comes, even if it seems unusual, strange or outside the "rules" of traditional meditative practices. Censoring and rejecting inner ideas can come from your ever evaluating, judging LB, pulling you off your center. Thank your inner mind for this gift and bring it to conscious awareness so you can learn to use it in the following exercise.

Many forms of meditation use a *mantra* to induce and maintain trance. A *mantra* is a sacred formula in the form of a word, phrase or chant repeated to oneself over and over to invoke divine quietness or power. Some people even pay hundreds of dollars for a "master" to give them a mantra. In EX 17 your own inner Master gives you a mantra, free of charge. Exercise 18 teaches you how to use it.

EX 18, USING YOUR MANTRA: This exercise is very much like EX 15. Instead of waiting for your next breath to come, wait for your next thought. Observe the space in between your thoughts. You can even count while you are waiting for a thought to come. When it does, simply see, feel, smell or repeat the "mantra" you got in EX 17. Your mantra will be an abbreviated form of self-talk, directing you and keeping you balanced and centered. It is not necessary to banish all thoughts from your mind, only to observe them. This is a no-lose exercise. You will either experience long periods of quiet (inner peace) or repeat your "mantra" often, invoking the divine within you. When you sense that it is time to stop this exercise, simply ask your Self, **"Have I absorbed what I need from my 'fertile void?' . . . am I ready to come out of trance or to move on to other trance 'work?' . . ."** The exact words given here are not important. Understand them and then use the words that come to you.

If you are an active, busy person, you may find the *thought* of EX 18 distasteful. You may think, I won't be able to stand doing nothing. It is surprising that when you suspend the "work-study-get-ahead-kill" dictums in your LB that drive you, you can actually enjoy the "nothingness" of inner quiet. From this place of stillness it is possible to observe your thoughts. When you are out of your center where thoughts come rapidly, you become your thoughts. They seem to control your mind and feelings, sapping you of your power. In the book cited in EX 16, Kay Cordell Whitaker's Shaman guides tell her (p. 48):

> Everyone hunts for power . . . some search for it through control of others. Some look in control of themselves. Some in righteousness. Others in magic. Almost nobody finds its hiding place. Where do you think it is?

As Ms. Whitaker discovers . . . power IS attention. Her guides tell her:

> Humans need to start paying attention to their attention." (p. 49) Our thoughts are part of where we scatter our attention and power . . . They crowd up the works, leaving little room for anything else the mind might do. (They) don't want to give up. They are afraid they will die. (In their own way) they're trying to take care of us. (p. 55)

Once you place your attention on your thoughts, they stop "thinking you" and you can heal them. You can turn their incessant monologue into a dialogue and allow truth to come by asking, "IS THIS A HELPFUL THOUGHT?

IS IT VALID? WHAT DO I GAIN FROM IT?" Sometimes, when you *think* you have no value, that you are hopeless, that you *have* to do something, . . . you are afraid to ask for inner guidance. You think your worst fears will be confirmed. However, truth is always freeing, releasing and ultimately leads to a sense of peace. Destructive habits of thought lead to anxiety, tension and disappointment. At this point, it is not necessary to know how to change these ancient thought patterns, but just to be able to use your Mantra to gently nudge them on.

Surprisingly, then, when you are centered, not only are you in a place of quiet, peace and comfort . . . you are also in a place of power! EX 19 uses imagery to help you maintain your center and create a vision of what resources you want to draw from it.

EX 19, SAFE PLACE: After you sense you have found your center by grounding, breathing and using your mantra, begin to search for a sort of tunnel that leads to the Center of your center. Without even knowing that you are already in this tunnel, you can find that you are walking, gliding or floating toward a tiny pinpoint of light that glows in a different way . . . And you will know if you are moving towards your place of peace, safety, comfort or power . . . because your Inner Realm can be any and all of these . . . You know that you do not need to know what this place will look like until you get there . . . It may be a place you have been before, or never been . . . an indoor place or outdoors or totally imaginary . . . Just allow yourself to be surprised and pleased by what you will find . . . And when you arrive in the soft glow of that inner place you can begin to explore it effortlessly with every sense that you have . . . noticing the colors, shapes, sounds, fragrances, textures, climate and karma of that world . . . You may want to continue to explore this place, perhaps finding a treasure to take back with you . . . or you may want to find a spot to rest where you savor everything that surrounds you and absorb what you need from it . . . And when you sense that you have found or gained what you require, you can begin the journey back through the tunnel towards the outer world, becoming ever more alert and wakeful as you leave . . .

EX 18 and EX 19 offer two different approaches to maintaining trances. The first uses a "mantra" to keep random thoughts from pulling you out of your center. The second uses imagery. Noticing the sights, sounds, textures, and temperature that make up a fantasy place is a way of remaining an observer and suppressing random thoughts.

Grounding and centering can certainly be an end in themselves. As energy simultaneously moves downward and inward a complete circuit is made where support and undiscovered resources flow. Establishing this connection may be all that you need from trance. But, your inner refuge is also a place of healing and growth. The rest of this book offers ideas for using trance towards those ends.

THE EXERCISES:

Trance "Work"

*D*iscovering your Inner Advisor

The purpose of this book is to deliver you to your Self. Within you is an "inner advisor" who has all the wisdom and strength you will ever need to deal with life's petty problems. This does not mean you should not go to others for help. During very difficult times it is easy to become cut off from this advisor. Sometimes you may need to connect with another person in order to get reconnected to your Self. Other minds can stimulate your own thinking, but beware of letting others think for you. Other's views can expand your own perspective, but always see through your own eyes. Fully digest any input you receive from others and then allow answers to come from within.

Your inner advisor is and always has been on call 24 hours a day waiting to guide you. You have probably had the experience of a thought coming to you, reminding you not to forget something important. That is your inner advisor talking to you. However, usually your inner guide does not offer unsolicited information.

When you do turn off the recordings that play over and over in your mind and ask your innermost Self a question, fresh answers can come. It is those loud, tyrannical habits of thought that shout "what-ifs," "if-onlys," "when-wills," "have-tos," "coulds," "shoulds," "awfuls," "terribles," "nevers," "always," "nobodies," "everybodies" over and over in your mind that make it difficult to hear your inner advisor.

Strangely enough, hard sobbing can make it easier to hear your inner guide—

> A man was fired from his job and he felt as though his life was over. He sobbed uncontrollably and his tears seemed to dislodge the "awfuls" and "terribles" that were terrifying him. As he continued crying, he became aware of something inside his mind saying, "Don't you know I've always taken care of you . . . " He did not have any religious faith and did not know what to make of that voice, but within 24 hours his "catastrophe" had been resolved.

It is difficult to identify exactly who or what that "voice" might have been, but the source of such inner calm deserves speculation.

Words lie. Your senses do not. At the same time that your loved ones, with the best of intentions, passed on misinformation when you were little, your senses were telling you the truth. The message that "Sex is Bad" may have been clearly recorded in your outer mind, but the pleasant, harmless sensations that came from touching your genitals were also stored in your inner mind. You may have been told countless times that you are weak, but unforgettable sensations of empowerment were recorded when you took your first step. Verbal recordings are prone to over-generalizations. If you had an abusive parent, you may have told yourself that people cannot be trusted. Yet, on a sensory level you (unawarely) noted tiny muscle movements, voice tenor, and subtle mannerisms that can help you discern actual danger. These are the truths that become available when you contact your observant Self.

The impressions you store in your inner mind may go deeper than your five senses. There may be an elusive "sixth sense" that allows your organism to realizes its inter-connectedness with everything in its environment and how completely it belongs in the grand scheme of things. With every breath of air you take and every drop of blood sugar that reaches your vital organs, your body "knows" that nature is sustaining it and taking care of it (even when you feel abandoned or doomed). And finally, there are those inexplicable incidents of Extra Sensory Perception, premonitions, and prophecy that suggest knowledge may come *through* your inner mind, as well as *from* it.

It is hard to have any conception of your wholeness when you are largely unaware of your inner mind. You can exhaust yourself struggling to solve problems with your outer mind, not allowing answers to come from within. But when your outer and inner minds *consciously* "work" together, the whole that is created is truly greater than the sum of its parts. It is in that conscious joining that your observant Self is born and reborn, over and over, every time the connection is made. It is your observant Self that is aware of conscious and unconscious processes, that understands and knows, that comprehends non-verbal sensory truths and dissolve false beliefs. When you balance the "see-saw" of your mind and come to rest in your center, you meet your Self.

You have already begun to invoke your inner guide by asking your Self questions suggested in various exercises in this book—

"What signs of relaxation am I noticing now?" (EX 2);

"Are my eyes ready to close n o w? . . . " "Just when will my eyes want to close? . . ." (EX 4);

"Are my eyes ready to stay closed or do they want to open? . . . " (EX 5);

"Do I need another breath yet? . . . " (EX 15);

"What picture, color, word, phrase, sound . . . represents what I'm experiencing now? . . ." (EX 17);

"Have I absorbed what I need from my quiet, no-thought place? . . . "

"Am I ready to come out of trance or to move on to other trance work? . . . " (EX 18)

Anytime you stop the monologue of LB mental chatter by sincerely asking your Self a question, a dialogue is begun that joins your two minds. You do not need to be in a trance to receive answers from the whole Self this dialogue creates. However, trance can make it easier to "hear" answers by suppressing distracting mental chatter. EX 20 gives steps for invoking your inner guide and using it to face your problems.

EX 20, INNER DIALOGUE: After entering trance (EX 8), grounding (EX 10-12) and centering (EX 13-16), use your mantra (EX 18) to stay with your quietness for a little while. When you sense you have gained what you need from your inner quiet, as suggested in EX 18, you can begin to hear answers within— **(a.)** Allow a question to come to your mind. Your question may be very open ended, **"What issue in my life would I like to address in this trance? . . . "** Such a question will not necessarily open Pandora's box. Your inner guide knows just the right time to address which problems. **(b.)** Whatever question you ask, simply wait for an answer to come. **(c.)** If you don't get an answer, enjoy the stillness. Your greatest need may be to use this trance for quiet peace and rest. Answers come in their own time. **(d.)** If you do get a specific answer, continue the dialogue with what ever questions occur to you. If the answer you get seems too hard, ask for clarification, **"How can I begin to do that? . . . "** **(e.)** Ask if there is any part of you that would object to following your advisor's guidance. Let your advisor know about this part's concerns and ask if it can suggest a way to meet that parts needs. **(f.)** See yourself practicing whatever behavior or attitude your inner voice suggests. Notice how you will be different in the future when you accept the guidance it gives you. When you sense that you understand what you need for now, you can begin to come out of trance. You may want to count up to five, bringing your energy upward to your outer mind as you do.

Martin L. Rossman, MD. in his book, *Healing Yourself,* describes another approach to meeting your inner advisor. If you have enjoyed the exercises in this booklet which utilize imagery (EX 12, EX 16, EX 19) or if you seem to have trouble "hearing" your still small voice in EX 20, Dr. Rossman's method may be more helpful to you. It gives symbolic substance to your inner guide, making it more personal, intimate and easier to access when you are not in trance.

EX 21, INNER ADVISOR: Begin with EX 19, traveling through you inner tunnel that leads to the center of your center. Let go of any previous images and discover if your "tunnel" leads you to the same or different place this time. After thoroughly exploring your new or old inner refuge with every sense you have, find a spot to rest and wait– **(a.)** Know that a presence can come to your inner realm that embodies your still small voice–the part of you that knows you well, completely understands you and cares for you deeply. This figure may be someone you have known in your past, someone you've never met, a shimmering light or an animal. Be attuned to changes in your inner realm, because your guide can take any form–a falling leaf, a hazy cloud, a different sound, a sea shell washed up on the beach. **(b.)** Accept what comes, as long as you can sense its caring and compassion. You can ask it, *"Are you here to help me? . . . Do you believe in me and love me? . . . "* Asking simple questions will help to begin the dialogue. You may even want to know its name. **(c.)** When you are ready, tell your inner guide about your problem and hear what it has to say. Ask questions for clarification of obstacles in the way that is suggested in EX 20. **(d.)** When you have the direction you need for now, begin to say good-by to your guide in whatever way your spirit leads you. Know that you can meet with your advisor again, whenever you wish. Find out the surest, easiest method for getting back in touch before parting. Begin your journey back through your tunnel, gaining renewed energy and confidence as you travel outward.

Some people prefer the direct approach of EX 20 of listening to their own still small voice, while others find it easier to discover their inner wisdom through the use of imagery as in EX 21. If you are not sure if you have met your inner advisor through EX 20 and 21, simply ask yourself who you would like for your own special guide. Pay attention to your first answer. It really doesn't matter if your guide is Smoky the Bear, Abraham Lincoln or the engine in your Trans Am. You can use imagery to conjure any friendly force that you trust to speak with truth and authority.

However, be aware that your inner voice will always speak in a way that leads to peace, relief and release. You may find yourself becoming tearful as you sense its love and listen to its simple wisdom. Even if you have committed some heinous act, it will not scold you . . . It can help you realize you are a good person who did something wrong and help you understand why you went astray. Any scolding or criticism comes from the tape recordings in your outer mind of human "advisors" who didn't know any better. Those recordings may be loud; but, once you make contact with your inner Self, its quiet authority will dispel past misinformation.

Working from an Internal Dialogue

You can tackle a whole host of problems simply by asking your inner advisor questions. The following list suggests ways to begin an *internal dialogue* that deepens trance, promotes self understanding and leads to simple remedies.

INSOMNIA: "What do I need to do right now to quiet my mind so I can sleep? . . . What can I tell myself to help me sleep through the night? . . ."

PAIN/ALLERGIES/ILLNESS: "Is there anything my pain or symptom is trying to tell me? . . . Is something contributing to my problem that I haven't realized yet? . . . What words or symbol would show me what is aggravating my problem? . . . What do I need to do or realize to begin to heal? . . . "

ANXIETY/WORRY: "What is making me feel anxious right now? . . . What do I need to understand to let go of this worry? . . . What do I need to remember when I start to feel panic? . . . "

HABIT CONTROL: "Is there any part of me that objects to my desire to stop smoking? . . . What need is that part attempting to meet through smoking? . . . What other ways could I meet that need than by smoking . . . Am I willing to use this new alternative instead of smoking to meet that need? . . . "

SELF CONFIDENCE: "What is the tape recording or false belief that keeps me from feeling good about myself? . . . What do I get out of holding on to that false belief? . . . What is the real truth about my goodness, desirability, belonging? . . . "

RELATIONSHIP CONFLICTS: "Why am I really upset with my partner (parent) right now? . . . Why is my partner (child) upset with me? . . . What gets in the way of my willingness to understand my partner? . . . .What do I need to understand in order to discover a solution to our conflict? . . . "

ABUSE: "Why do I keep blaming myself for what happened? . . . Am I in any way tarnished or less of a person because of what happened to me? . . . What do I need to do or understand to deal with the consuming anger I feel towards the person who abused me? . . . "

The above list is only a small sampling of the questions that can be used to begin an *internal dialogue* with your observant, knowing Self or advisor. Remember that the questions you ask are more important than answers you receive. When answers don't come, use questions during trance as a mantra (see p. 59) to block distracting thoughts and keep your attention focused on the troubling issue. The answer may come at surprising moments during your waking life because your inner mind is attuned to clues in your environment. Questions in themselves, are wonderful ways to plant indirect suggestions: **"What do I need to do right now to . . . quiet my mind so . . . I can sleep."**

As you read the above list, you may have noticed questions that you might be reluctant to ask. You might be afraid your inner guide will tell you something you don't want to hear. Conventional "wisdom" offers pat answers to complex problems. You might expect your inner guide to tell you to forgive, not forgive or confront a person who abused you. Yet, what you hear during trance is likely to be far more personal or creative than these cliché answers. The first step in dealing with consuming anger may simply be to acknowledge it, express it in a game of darts or to wink at your abuser each time you realize he or she no longer has power over you.

Forgiveness, confrontation and other easy answers are part of our solution oriented society that is looking for the quick fix. Although there are some "What-do-I-need-to-do" questions in the above list, they are well balanced by questions that focus on understanding— **"What do I need to understand, realize, know . . ."** Many people approach problems with the idea that they must be solved. However, difficulties have a way of "solving themselves" when they are thoroughly under-stood. Pearls of wisdom may be over looked by focusing on solutions rather than understanding what makes a problem a problem— **"What's hard for me about being corrected or criticized? . . . What is the real reason why my boss acts the way s/he does? . . . What do I need to remember about myself to be less hurt in these situations? . . ."** The questions and answers that come through a slow, focused trance dialogue will cre-ate a dance of their own that will lead you in the direction you need to go.

Using Imagery

Although an internal dialogue is a good way to con-nect your inner and outer minds and bring forth the powers of your observant self, it still relies on LB, verbal modes. Sometimes, in order to get past your usual ways of thinking, you will need to use the language of your sensing, inner mind. This is the language of pictures, symbols, images and sounds. Somatic problems are par-ticularly important to address in this manner, because raw sensory data is the language of the body. However, common, every day worries, beliefs, fears and even relationships can be represented through imagery.

An old Indian cure for headaches teaches an easy way to approach imagery. First notice exactly where your pain is located. Then think of a color and shape for your pain and ask yourself how much water (volume) it would hold. This process is repeated over and over. The head-ache seems to change and dissolve by giving it expres-sion through imagery. You can use exactly the same process to create images for thoughts. Stop reading just long enough to allow some random thought to come to your mind. Now ask yourself the following questions.

Let your mind be free and pay attention to the first ideas that come to you—

> **If this thought had a shape, what shape would it be? . . . How big might it be? . . . What would it weigh? . . . What color could it have? . . . Would it's texture be rough, smooth, fuzzy, polished? . . . What odor, taste and smell might it have? . . . What sound would it make? . . . Could this thought even be represented as an animal, object or type of cereal? . . .**

These sorts of questions can help loosen your mind by (freely) associating RB images with LB thoughts. They demonstrate that any problem, symptom, or issue can be represented through imagery. A hay fever attack may be transformed into a dripping faucet; daily worries may look like a pile of ants crawling all over each other; a difficult boss might appear as a barking dog and a husband may see himself as a jewelry case enclosing and protecting a valuable diamond (his wife). The steps outlined in EX 22 show how to play with imagery in a way that begins to transform problems at a whole different level.

EX 22, IMAGERY TRANSFORMATION: After entering trance, grounding and centering in your own familiar way, you can find yourself drifting through the tunnel that leads to the center of your center. Explore what ever place of power, comfort and/or tranquillity you find this time and discover a spot where you can rest and concentrate. When you sense you are ready, you can begin your imagery work— **(a.)** Focus your attention on the symptom or problem that has been bothering you. You may want to project the problem on a movie screen so you can stay detached from it and maintain a level of relaxation. **(b.)** Ask your Self for an image or symbol that would represent the problem. Accept whatever comes, whether it seems crazy, strange or trite. Fine tune the image. Make sure you can see it clearly. Examine it from different angles and distances. Explore its texture size and shape. **(c.)** Notice what's wrong with the image. How is it dysfunctional or what problem does it seem to be creating. You may even want to take a moment to understand why the image is having difficulty. **(d.)** Ask your Self what needs to happen to make this image work better or be less troubling. Watch the transformation take place. Use whatever resources you need to correct the image, no matter how fanciful or illogical. **(e.)** Compare the corrected image with the original problem image. Which is larger or more powerful? Take some time to strengthen the corrected image. You can even let it totally eclipse the first image. **(f.)** Repeat the transformation from the problem image to the corrected image a few times. Carefully notice how the change happens. Is it a sudden or gradual change? Become very adept at healing the "hurt" image in your mind. **(g.)** End the session by focusing intently on the healed image. Imagine that time is an illusion and that the change (in image) has already taken place. When you are ready, begin to move back through your tunnel towards your outer mind, feeling rested, alert and confident as you do.

Dr. Rossman in *Healing Yourself,* pp. 70-87, dis-
cusses this technique in greater depth. He points out that
images do not need to have medical accuracy to have a
healing effect. It is more important that they are person-
ally meaningful. In the examples above the "dripping
faucet" was carefully corrected with various sizes of
washers and wrenches and the allergy attack it represented subsided. The person overwhelmed with worries
became a soaring eagle looking at the pile of crawling
ants from greater and greater heights until her daily
problems seemed puny and insignificant. In the third
example, a man studied the barking dog to understand
why it was so unsettled and he found ways to approach
it. Over time, the husband no longer saw himself as a case
whose only purpose was to protect a valuable jewel and
realized he was more like a tree that had a vital ecological
role and was important to everything in its environment.

EX 22 is excellent to use when you are experiencing
levels of pain that make the concentration you need to go
into trance difficult. Begin with the first step, focusing
on the pain itself. Don't try to control your pain or ignore
it. Move into it. Allow an image to come that represents
your pain. You may even want to let the image get worse
because if you can learn to increase your pain, you can
also learn to decrease it. Continue with the steps outlined in EX 22. If your pain comes from a chronic
problem, work with your image regularly. You do not
always have to use the same image as you work with your
pain. Let other representations come freely to give you
more clues about what your body or spirit needs.

Before you change a symptom or problem, sometimes it is necessary to first find out if it has anything to
say to you or to make "peace" with it. EX 23 is adapted
from *Healing Yourself,* pp. 134-141 and Gestalt projec-

tive techniques. It combines both verbal and imagery modalities and allows the release of emotions that may be blocking progress. It may be best to do this exercise with a therapist or understanding partner.

EX 23, IMAGERY DIALOGUE: Begin as you did in EX 22 with steps **(a.)** and **(b.)** Then continue with the following steps—

(c.) As you pay attention to the image of your problem or symptom, notice what feelings you have towards it. Begin to express them in whatever way seems most appropriate. You can use words, gestures or noises. If you are working with a therapist or partner, let him or her represent your image and make eye contact. **(d.)** Then switch positions and become your image. Notice how you feel as the image and what thoughts you have. How do you look from the eyes of your image. What feelings does your image (of your symptom/problem) have towards you. Give your image a voice and express what it has to say, making eye contact if possible. **(e.)** Continue in this way, switching between yourself and your image. You will notice whether you're speaking as yourself or as your image. It can help to physically move positions. Ask your image what it wants from you and what it will do for you if you begin to meet its needs. **(f.)** Consider what your image wants. What issues or concerns would make it difficult for you to meet its needs. What tiny steps could you take towards satisfying its desires. If you cannot think of anything, ask for help from your inner advisor (EX 20 & 21). **(g.)** Let your image know any of the ways you've thought of that you could begin to meet its needs. Ask if it is willing to give you some relief as you start to give it what it requires. If it's not satisfied, find out what you could do in exchange for a little comfort. Continue to negotiate until you sense some movement or take a break. **(h.)** Finish the session by acknowledging what you have learned from your image and find a way to show appreciation of the contact you have had.

EX 23 can easily flow into EX 22. A woman discovers that her ferocious "Tiger" of an appetite needs regularly scheduled feedings before it can consider slowing its constant hunt for food. Gradually she learns to domesticate this tiger and finds it can purr with contentment as it begins to feel more satisfied in little ways. At the end of any healing and growth work always take time to see yourself or your image feeling and acting just the way you want (it) to be. This is the "map" your inner mind needs to navigate change.

Enhancing Sexual Enjoyment

Sexual enjoyment is one of those life "problems" that deserves special mention. If your sex life is absorbing, enjoyable, and fulfilling, you have already been practicing trance much more than you realize. Beyond procreation and pleasure, the purpose of sex may be to cleanse the mind of its constant mental chatter by focusing on the sensations of the moment. However, many people find their sexual experiences are lacking in some way. The methods you have learned to enter, maintain and use trance can be very helpful in the sexual arena. They are especially useful when sex has become dull and routine and can also be an important adjunct to any therapy for a sexual dysfunction. Problems in the bedroom stemming from unresolved relationship problems warrant other forms of counseling.

Sexual enjoyment is not about using the right techniques, finding better positions or learning the best places to touch. It is about suspending mental chatter, attending to bodily sensations, and following an inner direction about what movements or sounds want to be expressed. There is a natural rhythm in which the body charges from taking in stimulation and discharges sounds, movements and energy. The trick is staying focused on sensations during the charging phase. Just as focusing on a spot will naturally lead to eye closure (EX 4, EX 5), focusing on the sight of your partner's body, the sounds (and smells) of love making, and/or sensations of touch creates the choreography for the dance of love. Simply use your directed self-talk as you did in EX 3 to suppress distracting mental chatter.

> I'm noticing the lovely, furry texture of my partner's skin and how warm his body feels . . . I really like the way that touch felt and I'm aware of a sort of tingling, melting sensation . . . My breathing seems to be getting slower and deeper and it almost feels like I'm moving in slow motion . . . And now my body seems to want to move and push harder against my partner's . . . and I can feel him pushing back . . . And I'm aware of the rise and fall of his chest as he breaths . . . And I want to move with that rhythm . . .

People who are "sensors" and sensuous are very tuned in to the sights, sounds and textures of their environment. They do the above naturally and can stay focused on sensations without the use of self-talk. But people who are thinkers and preoccupied need to force themselves to tune in to sensory experiences. If your mind is very cluttered with the "business of life", it may be helpful to at least do EX 4 or EX 5 prior to love making to engage your automatic mind and begin to focus your attention. If your partner is willing to do this exercise with you, you can describe to each other your sensations of relaxation and discover how this can become a new type of foreplay. EX 24 shows how to carry "meditation foreplay" one step further.

EX 24, MEDITATION FOREPLAY: (a.) Lying next to or sitting across from your partner, use the methods that work best for you to enter trance, ground and center. **(b.)** You can find yourself drifting through the tunnel that leads to the center of your center, taking your partner with you to some special place of beauty and comfort . . . or you my find you have brought the very room or bed you are in now into your inner realm . . . Notice everything about your surroundings and take a moment to explore it in your mind . . . **(c.)** Watch what you and your partner do as you find each other in that inner place . . . how you move closer . . . how you first make contact . . . how a touch feels . . . what you want to do next . . . Let the dance of your love unfold before you . . . **(d.)** When you are ready, come back to outer reality or bring outer reality into your inner world so you can begin to make actual physical contact with your partner in any way your spirit leads you . . .

In their book, *Self-Hypnosis,* p. 256, Doctors Alman and Lambrou cite research showing that mentally rehearsing a skill (such as serving a tennis ball, shooting baskets, putting, or shooting billiards) actually improves the performance of that skill. There is no reason why mentally rehearsing making love cannot enhance that experience as well. Both partners can do EX 24 simultaneously and share their experience later, or one partner can lead the other through EX 24 in an interactive way:

EX 24, MEDITATION FOREPLAY: Partner: (a) "Focus your attention on a spot while you notice the signs of relaxation that begin to occur in your body . . . and when you've noticed one or two ways your body has become more quiet and still, (b) you can begin to really go inside yourself to some beautiful, pleasant place or even our very own bedroom and tell me what you are seeing" (other partner responds) . . . "Even if it's where we are now, describe to me what you see in your mind . . . What is the lighting like? . . . Tell me the colors and details of our surroundings . . . How are we dressed? . . . What do we look like? . . . Are there any sounds or music? . . . Can you detect any fragrances? . . ." (c) "How are we together? . . . Are we touching or looking at each other? . . . What do we start to do? . . . What is it like when I do that? . . . What happens next? . . . "

The partner leading the exercise can guide the fantasy through to its completion or it can flow easily into actual love making at the appropriate moment. Using imagery is important for people who need mentally arousing stimulation as well physical sensations to become absorbed in sexual experiences. Sexual fantasies are a well-known way to block distracting mental chatter. Using guided imagery has the additional advantage of involving the partners together in the creation of a fantasy. The book *Ordinary Women Extraordinary Sex* has more information about how to have "*trans*-cendent" sexual experiences and describes the heights of ecstasy some people have reached through finding their own "absorption style" and developing a "supersexual" mind-set.

Final Words

This book is meant as a beginning. Each person learns in his or her own way. You may want to work more with the exercises in this book on your own. As you read them over and over and continue to practice, you will make your own discoveries and develop your own techniques that can carry you far beyond these pages. Or, you may want a friend or therapist to assist you with what you are learning. You may discover that you have very deep hurts. These can best be healed by sharing them with someone who encourages their release in a way that "corrects" the original insult. Then trance can help you heal old wounds, digest the changes that are happening, and shed the *trappings* of personality that limit and confine your true self.

There is an old saying that "WHEN THE STUDENT IS READY, THE TEACHER WILL COME." Just as you found this book, you will find other guides that help show you the way towards continued growth. If you enjoy reading, the books described in the annotated bibliography may suggest clues you would like to pursue. But these last bits of advice you may or may not need to know. You are in good hands.

As you become more and more entranced with your Self, you can simply ask, **"Where do I need to go from here . . .?"** But do not be surprised if, sometimes, your answer is to stay . . . STILL . . . where you are . . . .

Metaphor of the Mind

Metaphor of the Mind

A metaphor is a special kind of image that stands for something else. Through metaphor you can reduce a problem to its essential components and discover new ways to manipulate it and bring about change. EX 22 teaches you how to create metaphors for problems, symptoms and issues in your own life. You will be amazed at the images that come to you as you begin to work with your problems on a symbolic level.

The following metaphor began as a way of dealing with mental states in which you are thinking so hard that it is difficult to focus your attention and begin to slow down. Its purpose is to induce trance through a metaphorical, indirect way. But it also offers one model for the elusive, almost

unfathomable concept of "mind." You may want
to use it as is; or you may need to fine tune it or
change it to deepen your own understanding of
"mind."

This is the one exercise in the book that you may
want to have read to you or that you may want to
record yourself. The language of trance is flowing
with pregnant pauses to allow time to focus
attention. Punctuation and italics are used to
suggest a different way of reading from your usual
speaking voice. As the reader, do not hesitate to
use long . . . lingering pauses and to change the
tone of your voice for special emphasis. As the
listener, simply focus your attention on a spot and
discover what happens . . .

There are times when you may find yourself in a
chamber buzzing with energy . . . A brightly lit room
filled with computers, printers, recorders, switch boards,
calculators, all conducting the business of life . . . And it
almost seems that you are one with the machines as they
sort, organize, analyze, record, retrieve data and relay it
to other chambers.

But the business of life . . . is not LIFE and even the
machines need . . . *down* time so you begin to wonder
where the . . . *off* switches might be. Strangely enough .
. . the floor of the chamber is on an upward incline, and
you notice a large lever on the other side of some open
windows at the upper end of the room . . . And even
though it takes effort, you are able to . . . *make your way
away* from the buzzing and clicking of the machines.

Your attention is drawn to the open windows which
flank both sides of the upper end of the room and offer

a panoramic view of the outer world . . . You notice other chambers which also seem strangely tilted upward as though suspended in space, separate and alone . . . And through those windows your can *hear* the noises . . . *feel* the breezes . . . *smell* the fragrances of the outer world. As you . . . *stare out* those observation windows, the whirring and busy-ness of the machines seems to recede into the distance . . .

So you become aware of the lever again . . . now within reach. As you slowly pull *down* on it, the chamber seems to right itself. It as though the room has moved upward into an enclosure which obscures the view from the observation windows but reveals an opening at the back end of the room . . . And you realize that the lever is indeed the . . . *off switch,* allowing only an occasional bleep to be heard from the computers . . .

As you . . . *move through* the back door opening, you realize you are now between the outer chamber you have just left and an inner chamber. From this middle place you have a clear view of both chambers . . . and you *turn your attention* to the back one. This second chamber has large movie screens where the windows were in the first. You can . . . *project any image you like* on those screens . . . And beyond them there seems to be a museum of sorts . . . where objects of art, statues and artifacts are strewn in no particular order.

You start to . . . *enter the back chamber*, but realize you are no longer over the center supports and that your weight has made the floor begin to tilt again. The floor of the inner chamber has started to . . . *slant downward*, and you look behind you to see that the outer chamber is lifting higher into the upper enclosure causing the opening between the two rooms to close off. Your own body seems to be losing weight and you notice that further down into the chamber objects are . . . *starting to float* as though the laws of gravity were strangely suspended . . . and that a kaleidoscope is starting to move at the far end where the computers were so busy in the outer chamber.

You know that if you go any further, you will become a part of that kaleidoscope and leave outer reality totally behind . . . So you come back to the middle ground between the two rooms where you can . . . view the inner chamber and . . . *stay balanced,* and where you have easy access to the outer chamber if you so desire . . . And so this center place seems to be a . . . *holding position* where the computers of the outer room are . . . *quiet* and the kaleidoscope in the inner room is . . . *still.*

With both chambers . . . *perfectly balanced,* you notice that you are lined up with a tiny opening at the far end of the inner chamber in the center of the kaleidoscope . . . It appears to be a black hole of great . . . *depth* that seems to lead far beyond your own inner chamber to exactly what you do not know . . . But if you attempted to move towards it, you know that the inner room would tilt downwards and passage beyond that chamber will disappear . . .

And although it takes . . . *quiet concentration* to . . . *remain balanced* and aligned with the openings to both chambers and beyond, you discover an amazing sense of . . . *peace* . . . As though that open channel you've revealed is a conduit through which . . . *inner calm can flow* . . . And with that calm can come . . . truths, knowledge, strength in whatever form you would like . . .

So you might . . . *invite an inner advisor* or guide to come to you who understands you completely, believes in you and cares deeply about you . . . And you can be surprised or pleased at whatever form this presence takes . . . Or you may just want to . . . *listen* for your inner "knowingness" with its simple truths.

So take a moment, now, to be with your inner guide or knowingness to . . . *find out* if there is anything you want or need from it, or if it has a special gift or message for you . . . And you can . . . *learn so much* in so little time because time changes when there are no boundaries . .

And when you . . . *gain the peace or understanding* for which you came, you can prepare to move back to the outer chamber . . . slowly moving the lever up, revealing the observation windows again . . . *taking time* to . . . *look through* them and enjoy the beauty of the outer world . . . before you return to conducting the business of life with what ever strength, energy, or clarity you need thoroughly replenished.

Coming to Terms

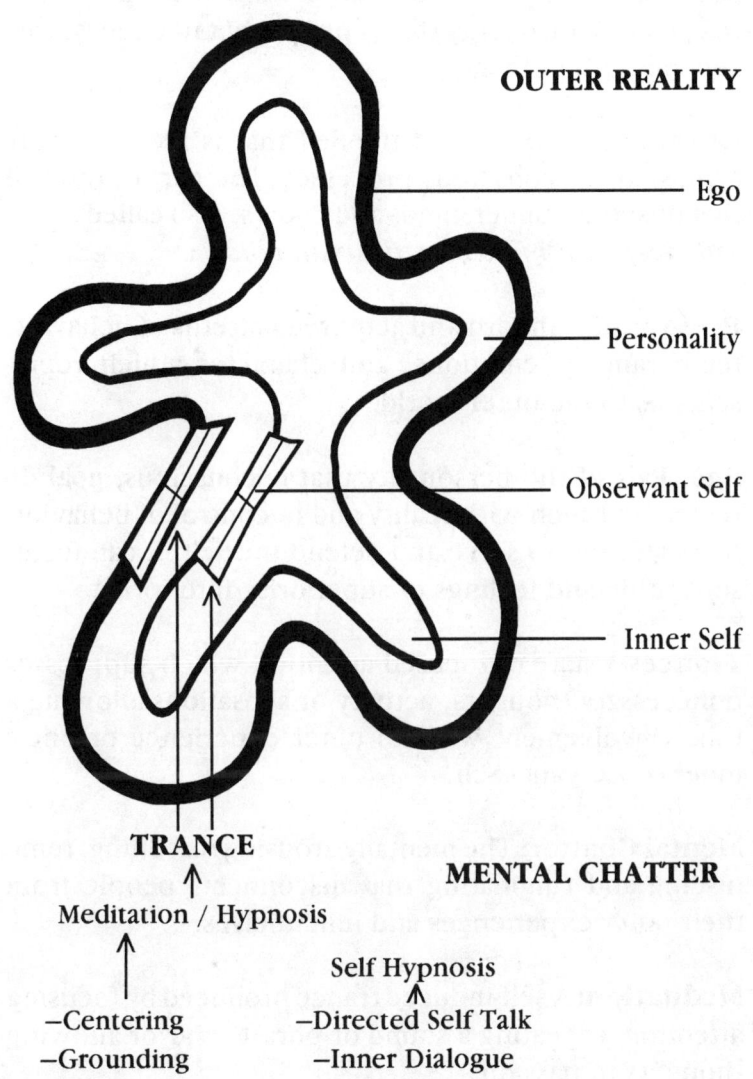

SELF

OUTER REALITY

— Ego

— Personality

— Observant Self

— Inner Self

TRANCE

↑

Meditation / Hypnosis

↑

—Centering
—Grounding

MENTAL CHATTER

Self Hypnosis
↑
—Directed Self Talk
—Inner Dialogue

Coming to Terms

Self: Totality of a person's being. Individual expression of (human) life energy that is unique but not necessarily separate from others.

Observant Self: Part of the Self that is aware of conscious and unconscious processes. The part of the Self that observes, understands and knows. Also called *inner self, deep self, knower, still small voice,* etc.

Personality: Inborn and acquired patterns of behavior, temperament, emotions, and character which represents us to the outer world.

Ego: Part of the personality that is conscious, goal directed, in touch with reality and in control of behavior. In its attempt to serve and defend the Self, it can foster separation and feelings of superiority/inferiority.

Trance: A state of focused attention which suppresses unnecessary thoughts, activity or sensations allowing a fuller involvement with an outer experience or one's inner (observant) Self.

Mental Chatter: The mentally arousing reasoning, reminiscing and ruminating that disconnects people from their outer experiences and inner Selves.

Meditation: A self-induced trance produced by focusing attention, repeating a sound or phrase, and/or allowing thoughts to pass on.

Grounding: The downward movement of energy in which it becomes absorbed into a larger source and forms a reciprocal, upward, revitalizing power flow. Experienced as heavy, sinking, or light, floating sensations.

Centering: The inward movement of attention in which mental activity in the brain cortex is suppressed and the calming center in the hypothalamus is activated. (See Pp. 18-19) Experienced as detachment, oneness or release.

Hypnosis: A method of inducing trance through predictions, observations, and indirect suggestion. Can be used to enhance personal functioning and solve problems.

Self-hypnosis: A self-induced trance produced by directed self-talk.

Directed self-talk: Making predictions, observations and indirect suggestions to yourself in a focused, repetitive way that suppresses random mental chatter.

Inner Dialogue: Directed self-talk in which the conscious, active mind asks questions and allows answers to come *through* the open, receptive subconscious mind which has access to repressed memories, uncontaminated (ego free) truths and mystical wisdom.

Topography of the Mind

BRAIN: Organ of the mind.

MIND: Totality of thought, perception, feeling, will, memory, sensation and imagination through which the Self operates.

Sub-Dominant Hemisphere (RB) *Subconscious mind functions:*	Dominant Hemisphere (LB) *Conscious mind functions:*
Ideomotor movement Catalepsy	Voluntary Motor Control
Observation	Perception
Imagery	Thought
Intuition	Reason
Emotion Catharsis or Abreaction	Logic
Knowledge	Beliefs
Free Association Revivification	Rumination Reminiscence
Dream (sleep) Fantasy	Day dreams

Sub-Dominant Hemisphere: Usually the *right* hemisphere of the brain that processes information nonverbally and simultaneously. It handles sensations, images, symbols, sensations, emotions and spatial relationships in order to synthesize,combine, create and express.
Subconscious mind: Part of the mind that controls our automatic, involuntary body functions. It receives and stores unorganized sensory and emotional impressions from our experiences below a level of awareness.

Ideomotor movement: Involuntary muscle movements that accompany inner images and thoughts, particularly when voluntary motor control is absent.
Catalepsy: Involuntary suspension of normal muscle response to commands or external stimuli. Occurs during dream states or through suggestion in trance.

Observation: Raw data noticed or perceived directly through the senses or an instrument.

Imagery: Mental impressions of sensory input that are seen, heard, smelled, tasted or felt in the mind.

Intuition: Knowing without using thoughts or reason. Perceived as inner seeing, listening or feeling from processing subtle cues and connections. Similar to *insight,* or spontaneous understanding.

Emotion: Involuntary muscular tensions and hormonal reactions to thoughts (often irrational) experienced in different parts of the body and given a subjective feeling label.
Catharsis or **Abreaction:** Release of emotions and related muscular tension through crying, laughing, talking, raging, sweating, shaking, and yawning.

Knowledge: Information gained directly with the senses or mind. To understand with clarity and certainty. Similar to *discernment.*
Free Association: Spontaneous process in which stored images, symbols, sensations, emotions and thoughts that are linked in some way trigger each other.
Revivication: The experience of reliving a past memory with associated emotions, sensations, and images. Can occur spontaneously in a flashback or through suggestion during trance.

Dream (sleep): A scenario in which sensations, images, symbols and emotions are combined in illogical and disjointed ways.
Fantasy: A scenario that uses mental imagery and has little or no story-line.

of the Mind

Dominant hemisphere: Usually the *left* hemisphere of the brain that processes information verbally and sequentially. Uses words, numbers, and abstract concepts to analyze, reason and reach conclusions. It turns thoughts into action through voluntary motor movements.
Conscious mind: Part of the mind that controls our deliberate, voluntary, intentional thoughts and actions. It organizes and stores verbal recordings of our experiences at a level that is accessible to awareness.

Voluntary motor control: Intentional, purposeful gross muscle movement directed by conscious thoughts and desires (commands).

Perception: Interpretation, representation, or understanding of direct observations.

Thoughts: Mental activity involving words, numbers or concepts.

Reason: The process of reviewing and sorting through accessible information in order to analyze, assess, evaluate, make decisions, reach conclusions and solve problems.

Logic: The art or principles of reasoning. Reasoning that is valid or accurate in which thoughts are consistent and rationally related.

Beliefs: Conclusions about a situation, person or event arrived at through the process of thinking and reasoning. Similar to *opinions, values, assumptions.*
Rumination: The process of examining troubling thoughts over and over again with no clear purpose in mind. Similar to *worrying* and *obsessing.*
Reminiscence: The process of consciously reviewing and recollecting a past experience through words and images.

Day Dream: A goal-oriented scenario using words and images in which the "dreamer" accomplishes some end.

Bibliography

Alman, Brian M. Ph.D. and Peter Lambrou, Ph.D. *Self-Hypnosis, The Complete Manual for Health and Self-Change*. New York: Brunner/Mazel, 1992. Multitude of suggestions, examples and scripts for self-hypnosis.

Benson, Herbert, M.D. *The Relaxation Response*. New York: Avon Books, 1975. A doctor explains the physiology of meditation and how it can be used in stress-related diseases.

Bloch, George, Ph.D. *Body & Self, Elements of Human Biology, Behavior, and Health*. Los Altos, CA: William Kaufmann, Inc., 1985. Explains interactions between our bodies and minds.

A Course in Miracles, Tiburon, California 94920: Foundation for Inner Peace, 1975. A curriculum for spiritual growth. Esoteric style can be difficult to read but has its own special beauty.

Hittleman, Richard. *Richard Hittleman's Yoga, 28 Day Exercise Plan.* New York: Bantam Books, 1969. Four-week exercise plan with clear instructions and pictures.

Rossman, Martin L., M.D. *Healing Yourself, A Step-by-Step program for Better Health Through Imagery.* New York: Pocket Books, 1987. Explores mind/body connection to show how to unleash the body's natural healing powers.

Scantling, Sandra, Dr. and Sue Browder. *Ordinary Women Extraordinary Sex.* New York: Penguin Books USA Inc., 1993. Describes the nature of "transcendent sex" and therapeutic approach for achieving same.

Whitaker, Kay Cordell. *The Reluctant Shaman.* San Francisco: Harper Collins Publishers, 1991. Auto-biographical account of Ms. Whitaker's "reluctant" apprenticeship to two shamans from the Amazon Basin.

Wolinsky, Stephen, Ph.D. *Quantum Consciousness.* Connecticut: Bramble Books, 1993. Over 80 exercises to explore and experience the quantum approach to problem resolution.

About the Author

Kate Cohen-Posey, M.S. LMHC LMFT has been a therapist practicing in Polk County, Florida since 1973. The literature she has written for clients over the years has provided a medium for artistic expression of her therapeutic skills. The popularity of her writing with clients and colleagues has encouraged her to reach a wider audience. It is her aim to develop concise, easy-to-read materials that assist and shorten the therapeutic process OR provide a means of independent study for those who wish to further their own emotional / spiritual development.